15-Minut

GW00818375

Reducing the Stress Factor

Dr Bill and Frances Munro

Copyright © CWR 1996, 2002, 2003
First published 1996 as *A Place of Rest: Reducing the Stress Factor*, by CWR.
This edition published 2002 by CWR, Waverley Abbey House, Waverley Lane, Farnham,
Surrey GU9 8EP.
Reprinted 2002, twice in 2003.

Concept development, editing, design and production by CWR.

All rights reserved. No part of this publication may be reproduced, stored in a retrieval
system, or transmitted, in any form or by any means, electronic, mechanical, photo-
copying, recording or otherwise, without the prior permission in writing of CWR.

Unless otherwise identified, all Scripture quotations in this publication are from
the Holy Bible: New International Version (NIV). Copyright © 1973, 1978, 1984,
International Bible Society.

Printed in England by Halstan
ISBN 1-85345-206-8

Biography

Dr Bill Munro was head of Medical and R&D Operations for a major pharmaceutical company and Medical Director for another. He is an Occupational Health Physician, was a consultant with many international companies, and Regional Officer for the Post Office.

Frances Munro is a pharmacologist. Her experience includes work with scientific staff recruitment and in clinical research management within the pharmaceutical industry, especially in the area of psychotropic medicines. She holds a diploma in counselling and had an extensive counselling and counsellor supervision practice.

They have written other books on stress: **Designer Living, The Way to Beat Stress**, originally published by Monarch and reprinted by SALT (Stress and Life Trust); **Beat Stress – a 30 Day Programme**, originally published by HarperCollins and reprinted by SALT; **Stress Facts and Action Plan**, published by SALT.

Bill and Frances founded SALT (Stress and Life Trust) in 1989. SALT runs seminars and provides coaching and consulting on stress prevention and management for secular and Christian organisations and individual churches.

Action Man – or Woman

A few years ago, doctors who ran a heart clinic in America noticed that many of the chairs in their waiting room were getting worn out along the front edge. They started to observe patients in the waiting room and found that many of them sat right on the edge of their chairs, poised for action, hence the wear and tear on this part of the chairs. This led them to look more deeply into the behaviour of their heart patients.

Living in the fast lane

They found that many of them were action people, and they termed their behaviour Type A. Such people live in the fast lane; drive fast, eat fast, talk fast. They are impatient; flash their lights behind you on the motorway, finish your sentences for you; always under time pressures; it gives them a buzz and they love it; they seem hooked on adrenaline. Not for them a relaxing holiday on the beach. They go scuba diving or hang gliding or hire a car and visit all things of interest in a 50-mile radius. They feel guilty doing nothing.

They cannot do just one thing at a time. They read while they eat. Eat while they work. Work on their computers while talking to you on the phone. They are often workaholics and can be very ambitious, not just for themselves, but for their department, organisation or church. They are perpetually on the go and are delighted to tell you how pressured they are.

There is nothing wrong with using time profitably or working hard, within reason. But there is bound to be wear and tear on the individual who is overdoing it. More recent research suggests that Type As who are also AHA types – Angry, Hostile and Aggressive – are particularly prone to heart problems.

> **"Be still, and know that I am God."**
> **Psalm 46:10**

Type A people

Are you a Type A, or married to one, or know one, or work for one? Many chief executives and directors of organisations are Type A. They can cause problems for those who work for them. Not only do they drive themselves, but everyone else too. They are very goal-orientated and because of this are often not very people-orientated. They can be pushers rather than leaders.

We need you, Type As. Your organisation needs you. Your church needs you, but please, without the toxic element of your behaviour which can hurt others and your own health.

The Lord Jesus was the most balanced man who ever lived. He was not under time pressures. Despite all the demands on Him, He had time to spend with His Father, with His disciples, and alone. He preached to large crowds but had time to stop and speak to individuals. Is there not a lesson here for those of us who are Type A?

For reflection and action:

* Are you driven? An action man or woman?
* Do you need to slow down?
* Should you be spending more time with the Lord, "listening to Him", and building relationships with your family, friends and your staff?
* Have you thought about a retreat? Wow! I dare you!

If anxiety and stress is under control, then it actually helps you to perform better, to tackle a problem, to motivate you to try harder, to work on that relationship. But if the anxious feelings are severe and over the top, they may ruin your performance. They may affect your behaviour. You can't think straight or make decisions. Prolonged or severe anxiety and stress can go on to affect our bodies and we can develop medical conditions which our doctor may tell us are due to stress.

How do I cope?

When you are very anxious, all you want is to get rid of the terrible feelings. I wonder how you cope with anxiety. Do you try to tell yourself that you're not anxious? Do you try to ignore it? Do you want to run away? Do you keep busy all the time? Try to forget it? Go and exercise? Take tranquillisers? Eat more? Smoke more? Drink more?

You may have prayed or asked for prayer that God will take away the anxious feelings. Whatever you do, the anxiety may remain, or it may go away for a time and then return, or may even get worse. Why?

The problem is that the anxiety is only a symptom – a sign – that something is wrong. It is like the red light on your car dashboard coming on. You would not, if you are wise, ignore the warning light, try to cover it up or try to forget about it. You would not, I hope, even pray that God would make it go out. No, the red light is there to alert you that there is a fault, that you should try to find out why the red light has come on, and then deal with the fault.

It is important, therefore, for us to know something of how anxiety develops. We are apt to think that something happens or there are circumstances which make us feel anxious. But this is not usually so.

> **"For as [a man] thinketh in his heart, so is he."**
> **Proverbs 23:7 AV**

Shakespeare wrote in *Hamlet*: "There is nothing either good or bad but thinking makes it so." Hans Selye – the father of stress medicine wrote: "It is not what happens to you that matters, but how you take it." Charles Swindoll, Christian author, wrote: "I am convinced that life is 10% what happens to us and 90% how we react."

Faulty thinking

In other words, anxiety is not the result of what has or is happening, but the result of how we interpret what is happening, what we think about things, what we believe about them, how we "see" them, how we react. If one man coming up to retirement thinks of all the opportunities it will bring, he will feel good about it. If another thinks about all the drawbacks, less money, too much time on his hands, no longer any status, he may feel stressed about it.

You cannot change your anxious feelings. The secret is that you need to find out what thinking has led you to feel anxious, to identify where the thinking is faulty and then change it – the feelings will then change.

Is all this psychobabble? I don't think so. Tomorrow we will see what Scripture has to say and the steps we must take to deal with anxiety.

For reflection and action:

* *Anxiety is due to our thinking, not circumstances or what is happening to us.*
* *How do you deal with your anxiety?*

7

Anxiety 2

Your feelings of anxiety are determined by your thinking, your beliefs, your interpretation of events, how you see them. St Paul says, "*Be transformed by the renewing of your mind*" (Romans 12:2). If we do not think "correctly" about things and our thinking is worried, then we will feel anxious and this in turn will determine how we act.

When Moses sent the 12 spies into the promised land, they all saw the same things. Two of them came and reported that the land was full of giant fruit, but the other ten reported that the land was full of giants. You know the result. Because of this thinking, the people were afraid and did not invade the land, but instead, wandered for 40 years in the wilderness.

When I was about to take early retirement as Regional Medical Officer for the Post Office to establish SALT, I was sitting at home one evening feeling anxious. Frances, my wife, asked why I was looking anxious. "I am worried about how we are going to make ends meet when I have given up my job."

"Would you feel as anxious if you had one million pounds in the bank?"

"Oh no", I replied.

"Bill, do you believe that the God you serve owns the cattle on a thousand hills? Do you believe that He will let you go without what you need for us and the family?" I paused. Did I really believe that? Did I really think that?

I said "Yes, I believe that. That is what I think". Within moments the anxious feelings had gone, because I had begun to think as I should.

Dealing with anxiety

So next time you feel anxious, here are the steps I believe you need to take:

1. Admit to yourself and to God that you are feeling anxious. If you try to hide the feelings, suppress or repress them, they may come out in some other way, shape or form – either as a mental condition, or perhaps as a medical condition.

2. Work through, either yourself or with the help of someone you trust, what your thinking is about the situation or the event. Is your thinking exaggerated, emotive, not very rational or just plain silly. Is your thinking biblical? Are you believing God. Are you trusting Him. Anxiety can be lack of faith in disguise.

3. Repent of the faulty thinking (not of the feelings – they are only the product of the thinking).

4. Decide what your thinking should be as a Christian. If you are not sure, ask God to reveal this to you.

5. Resolve to change your thinking to be in line with God's Word. If you find it difficult to change your thinking, then tell God that you are willing for Him to change it.

6. Continue to think according to God's Word.

Your feelings of anxiety should go.

"... we take captive every thought to make it obedient to Christ" (2 Corinthians 10:5).

For reflection and action:

* Are you anxious?
* Try, with God's help to determine what your thinking is. Is it faulty; unbiblical?
* Ask God to reveal what it should be and how to change it.

Not Belonging

Do you remember as a child when sides were picked for a game and you were left out? When others got invitations to parties and you didn't; St Valentine's Day when others got cards and you did not. You felt that you did not belong, and that is very stressful.

Feeling rejected

Everyone needs to feel that they belong and when you don't you feel rejected and your self-image is damaged. And people with a poor self-image do not cope well with pressures and stress.

The need to feel that we belong starts right from birth. Babies need to feel that they belong to a mother or whoever is caring for them. If they do not feel this then they can fail to thrive. It goes on into childhood and adolescence. But we have a problem if it goes on into adulthood. At work we need to feel part of the team or department. If we do we are happier and work better. Even in our church, we can feel that we do not belong, that we are being ignored, passed over, marginalised.

Needing to belong, and the rejection when we do not, permeates our life. We can blame others. We may try to ignore the feelings. We can move. This may make us feel better temporarily, but we may go on being rejected and feeling that we do not belong, that we are unacceptable.

There are more positive, lasting and biblical ways of dealing with this, but first there are a number of things we have to accept. First, people let other people down. Our enemies, our friends, and even other Christians may reject us, either knowingly or thoughtlessly. Secondly, there will be times in the world when we will not belong and we have to accept this. Thirdly, even if we feel that we do not belong, this does not make us unacceptable. All it means, quite simply, is that we feel rejected.

> **"Yet to all who received him, to those who believed in his name, he gave the right to become children of God – children born not of natural descent, nor of human decision or a husband's will, but born of God."**
> John 1:12–13

What then should we do?

Remember and learn from the Lord Jesus. People rejected Him. He did not belong. *"He came to that which was his own, but his own did not receive him"* (John 1:11). Did He get annoyed with them? Did He reject them in return? Did He wash His hands of them? Did He defend Himself? Did He stop loving them? No, no. He said *"Father, forgive them, for they do not know what they are doing"* (Luke 23:34).

It is important that you do forgive those who have rejected you, that you go on loving them and praying for them. You may need to ask for God's grace to do this. Remember, too, that though all may leave you or reject you, Jesus never will. Remember that you do belong. You belong to God. You are His child. He is your Father. Jesus is your Brother. You belong to God's family. Even if you feel that you do not belong in a church or fellowship, you do – by divine right.

For reflection and action:

* *Do you feel that in some part of your life you do not belong?*
* *Do you need to give up using the coping mechanisms which may make you feel better temporarily?*
* *Do you need to forgive those you think are responsible for you not belonging?*
* *Tell yourself the truth about Who you belong to and why.*

Blame

We live in a culture of blame. Always the cry is "Whose fault is it? Who was to blame? Who should be punished?" Graffiti on a Chicago subway stated, "Humpty Dumpty was pushed." Manufacturers in the USA are so afraid of being sued if something goes wrong with their products, that they go to extreme lengths to try to protect themselves. I learned about a child's buggy which had a notice on it: "The child should be removed from this pushchair before it is folded up." Presumably a parent somewhere had started to fold it with the child still in, to the discomfort of the child, and had then sued! This may be an extreme case, but we constantly hear interviews on TV asking someone, "And who's to blame, who do you think is responsible for this?"

Resentment = danger

Certainly, when things go wrong and we have a complaint or a legitimate claim, then we should be able to be heard and be justly compensated. However, if we continue to blame others, harbour resentment and grudges, this can affect our mind and our bodies.

An interesting question was posed in a study of survivors from a number of recent disasters who were suffering from Post Traumatic Stress Syndrome. Should survivors forgive and forget, or should they blame and rage against those who may have injured them? This is a situation we often see on TV programmes when survivors are being interviewed. There may be anger at the government, or the insurance company, legal personnel or the media, the rescue or medical personnel. Anger is greatest when justice does not seem to have been done following the disaster. The cry is, "Someone should pay for this."

Studies have shown that the more a victim blames another person for the accident, the more poorly he copes. In one study it was shown that those who took responsibility for the problems created by the accident had fewer stress-related difficulties than those who blamed others.

The need to forgive

Anger and bitterness can go on for years. Being unforgiving, angry, resentful and bitter is wrong in God's eyes, but it can also damage our minds and bodies and delay recovery. We are told to forgive and not to harbour bitterness. *"Get rid of all bitterness, rage and anger, brawling and slander, along with every form of malice. Be kind and compassionate to one another, forgiving each other, just as in Christ God forgave you"* (Ephesians 4:31, 32). It may be difficult, almost impossible to do in our own strength, and often we will need God's help and grace to do it, but do it we must if we do not want to be damaged ourselves.

Even more important, we must forgive so that we may be forgiven – *"And when you stand praying, if you hold anything against anyone, forgive him, so that your Father in heaven may forgive you your sins"* (Mark 11:25).

For reflection and action:

- Are you harbouring resentment or a grudge?
- Is there someone you need to forgive?
- Love keeps no record of wrongs (1 Corinthians 13:5).

Complaining vs Confiding

A large study in America looked at how hospital laboratory scientists coped with stress. The first two things they felt they should do were "confront the pressure" and "engage in exercise or sports activity". But top of the list for what they actually did was "complain to someone". (Interestingly, "pray" came about half way down a list of 23 coping mechanisms – both what they felt they should do and what they actually did.)

We all complain about someone, or something. We feel better, at least temporarily. It may change things when we complain, but often it doesn't. It makes other people defensive and antagonises them. If it becomes a way of life, it makes us bitter and unforgiving; things which are bad for us emotionally, physically and spiritually.

Confiding helps ...

There is a crucial difference between confiding and complaining. Confiding helps. Studies have shown that women who do not have a confiding relationship, especially with a husband or boyfriend, are more vulnerable to depression, and individuals who do not have an intimate confiding relationship are more likely to become depressed when faced with a big life pressure.

One of the reasons God has put us in families, and in the extended family of the church, is because confiding in one another helps. We are told to bear one another's burdens. We can also confide in the Lord. "*I sought the Lord, and he answered me; he delivered me from all my fears ... This poor man called, and the Lord heard him; he saved him out of all his troubles*" (Psalm 34:4, 6). This is different from complaining to God. God is not keen on us complaining, after all He has done for us and continues to do for us, and especially if what we are complaining about He has especially designed to teach or refine us.

... complaining doesn't

In the wilderness the Israelites "complained about their hardships in the hearing of the Lord, and when he heard them his anger was aroused. Then fire from the Lord burned among them and consumed some of the outskirts of the camp" (Numbers 11:1). And later, when they complained about the manna which God had provided, *"The Lord became exceedingly angry, and Moses was troubled"* (v.10). *" You want meat,"* the Lord said, *"I will give you meat. You will not eat it for just one day, or two days, or five, ten or twenty days, but for a whole month – until it comes out of your nostrils and you loathe it – because you have rejected the Lord ..."* (vv. 18,19,20).

Boy, was God angry. Yes, He is a loving God, but I think we have to think twice before we complain about our circumstances or our lot. I get worried when I hear people saying "I got angry with God". It's when He gets angry with us that we have to look out.

For reflection and action:

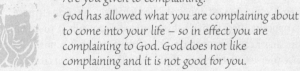

- Are you given to complaining?
- God has allowed what you are complaining about to come into your life – so in effect you are complaining to God. God does not like complaining and it is not good for you.

Changing Others

"How can he not see that what I am saying is right?" "How can she not see that she should do as I am suggesting?" "How can they be so stupid?" How often have you heard people saying things like this? How often have you said it yourself? We all want people to change.

In Northern Ireland, Bosnia, Rwanda, people want others to change and agree with them. In our community and country we want people to vote the way we do and have the same priorities – and prejudices.

We want our children and teenagers and spouse to agree with us; to like the music, the TV programmes, the books, the church we like, to have the same values as us. We want colleagues at work to agree with us. We want other Christians to believe what we believe and worship the way we worship. If only we could change everyone so that they were just like us!

You can't make them change

If you have ever tried to convince people they should change, you will know how stressful it is, especially if they don't and persist in going on thinking and doing it their way. You get frustrated when they don't comply and dig their heels in. You get annoyed when what you say seems to have exactly the opposite effect from what you wanted. Eventually, if you're not careful, your anger can turn to abuse, or you may wash your hands of them. You can save yourself a lot of stress if you learn that you cannot change anyone unless he or she is willing to be changed.

If you have young children, or have observed others, you will know that apart from physically restraining them, you cannot make them do what you want them to, let alone change how they think about something. They have to learn for themselves – it is part of the process of growing up. This can be clearly seen in adolescents as they move from dependence on us and learn to be more independent.

> **"Accept one another, then, just as Christ accepted you,
> in order to bring praise to God."**
> **Romans 15:7**

Your spouse, your colleagues, your fellow Christians and fellow church members are as entitled to their opinions and way of doing things as you are. Hopefully they will grow and develop as people and as disciples as they listen to you and then learn for themselves. They may get hurt on the way and you will have to bite back the "Well, I told you so".

If you don't want to get stressed when others don't listen or don't change – what should be your strategy? I do not believe you should opt out by not voicing your opinion in the best way you can, or not doing what you believe should be done.

Leave it to God

If you believe it is God's truth, then you should say it or deal with it with boldness, yet humility and love, in a way that will please and glorify God. You may have to point out that if they do not change, there may be consequences. You cannot make them change, so do not make it your objective. Leave the outcome to God. He will not hold you responsible if they do not change, but He will hold you responsible for what you said or did, and how, and why, and whether you kept on and prayed that His will would be done.

For reflection and action:

* *Are you trying to change someone?*
* *Should you be leaving the outcome to God?*

Caring for Others

Would you like to learn a proven way of reducing your stress and raising your immunity? Caring for and being responsible for others will do this. This may be one reason why married men live longer than single men. Apart from the care and attention they get from their wives, they are responsible for others. You have to be careful here, because too much responsibility can reduce immunity and be stressful.

Looking after the fish!

Much work has been done on the good effects on health of having a pet. There may be many reasons for this. Stroking a pet can lower blood pressure. Pets – especially dogs – give us "non-evaluative support". But beyond this, one of the reasons why we benefit is that we are responsible for them. Even looking after fish can benefit us in this way.

Believe it or not, but being responsible for plants has similar benefit. Several studies have proved this. In one old people's home, some of the old people were given responsibility for the plants in their rooms and others were not. The ones who were remained healthier for longer. Patients recovering from surgery in one surgical ward were put in charge of the plants. In another ward the staff tended the plants. The recovery rate where the patients cared for the plants was much quicker than in the other ward, and they were able to leave hospital earlier.

There is much teaching in Scripture about caring for others. The most well-known is the story of the Good Samaritan. Other examples are: "*If you really keep the royal law found in Scripture, 'Love your neighbour as yourself,' you are doing right*" (James 2:8); "*Carry each other's burdens, and in this way you will fulfil the law of Christ*" (Galatians 6:2); "*Encourage the timid, help the weak*" (1 Thessalonians 5:14).

> **"The entire law is summed up in a single command:**
> **'Love your neighbour as yourself.'"**
> **Galatians 5:14**

Obviously, caring for others will benefit them. But as long as it is not too much for you, you can benefit too: *"Blessed is he who is kind to the needy"* (Proverbs 14:21).

"But when you give to the needy, do not let your left hand know what your right hand is doing, so that your giving may be in secret. Then your Father, who sees what is done in secret, will reward you" (Matthew 6:3).

If you are part of a family you may already have a lot of responsibilities and you may have to be careful that you do not take on too many, because this can be stressful. If you are alone and do not have family responsibilities, you could perhaps "adopt" someone in your church.

You may live on your own and find it difficult to care for others. But there are ways. You can give directly, or to a charity, either time or money. You can write a letter of encouragement: *"Like cold water to a weary soul is good news from a distant land"* (Proverbs 25:25). It will also benefit you, especially if you undertake to write regularly.

You can pray for others. *"After Job had prayed for his friends, the Lord made him prosperous again and gave him twice as much as he had before"* (Job 42:10).

Caring for and being responsible for others can benefit you.

For reflection and action:

- If you do not have too many responsibilities, should you be taking on a family pet, or caring for others?

Don't Jump to Conclusions

You can save yourselves a lot of stress by taking your time: time to ponder, time to pray, and when you learn or hear things, by not jumping to conclusions which may well be wrong.

Sometimes, others do not express themselves too well, sometimes we do not interpret what they say too well. Sometimes others do things and we wrongly guess their intentions.

But I thought you meant ...

Some years ago I went to work for a pharmaceutical company in Holland. The medical department was truly international and had attracted some quite brilliant men from all over the world. I was rather overawed in my first days there as I realised what might be expected of me. The head of the department, a Dutchman, invited me to sit in on a meeting with his administrator, a Yugoslav, about a programme of research for a new drug. They discussed, in English, the way forward. The administrator then paused: "Should we involve Dr Munro in this programme?"

"No," was the reply, "he does not have the intelligence"!!

My face fell. I had only been here three days. How did they know already that I did not have the intelligence? Was my career in the pharmaceutical industry finished before it had begun? What would I do now? They would obviously not want to keep me on. How could I face my family? I had uprooted them from England to start a new life here. How could I face colleagues back home? I did not hear any of the rest of the discussions on the research plan for the new drug. I had a sleepless night and wondered when I would be given my marching orders. Surprisingly, the next day, the head of the department was extremely nice to me ("Just being a polite Dutchman") but also gave me work to read to familiarise me with certain of the programmes, including the one we had discussed the day before.

Stop and think

I kept on thinking, however, about "He does not have the intelligence". Eventually, and slowly, the penny dropped. He had been using the word "intelligence" not to describe my IQ, but what I knew about the programme, what information I had of it – like that branch of the army called the "Intelligence Service" which picks up information. As I began to believe that, much of my stress disappeared and I was able to concentrate on the work and not on my anxieties and fears.

In fact, I spent three happy years working in the department in Holland. What a difference it made when I took time to stop and think and interpreted what had been said correctly (at least I hope I had!).

For reflection and action:

- *Are there stresses in your life because you have jumped to conclusions?*
- *Might these conclusions be exaggerated or even wrong? Do you need to ask God for His wisdom in reinterpreting them and dealing with them.*

The Custard Principle and Stress

I wonder if you have heard of the custard principle? It's one of the principles we give on our seminars on Stress Prevention and Management. Quite simply it is: "Don't get upset over trifles". The American version is: "Don't sweat the small stuff".

"The hassle factor"

Do you get stressed over the unimportant things – small things – sometimes known in stress research circles as "the hassle factor"? Is it worth it? The answer must be "No" when you realise the harmful effects such anxiety can have on your emotional, mental and physical well-being. When I have found myself fretting or getting anxious over small things, I have sometimes asked myself, "Would someone who has been through the holocaust be worrying about this? Or someone who survived years in a Japanese P.O.W. camp? Would someone who has just come through major surgery or cancer be letting this get them down?" No, they all will doubtless be so glad to have survived such ordeals and to be alive that most other things will be small and insignificant in comparison.

Changed perspective

Conversely, the quickest thing to stop us worrying over trivia is to be suddenly confronted with a very big and important event or tragedy in our lives. Our perspective quickly changes.

I remember a very nice man consulting me over a period of time for a number of minor medical and emotional problems. He was really a bit of a hypochondriac and worried about every symptom he had. Together we explored these and my patient agreed that they were not serious and probably were stress related. Despite this recognition he kept coming to see me for reassurance and support. Then one day he had a stroke which badly paralysed him down one side. He made valiant efforts to overcome this disability and would not give in. Then I realised that it was weeks, and on into months since I had heard about any of the previous complaints. Now he had a bigger and more important concern. This had taken his mind off the small complaints.

My own present pressures and problems pale into insignificance when I think of the suffering and terrible trials that people are going through in certain parts of the world at this time, and I have to ask God to forgive me for getting upset over trifles.

For reflection and action:

* *Have you been getting stressed over small things, things that, at the end of the day, do not matter much?*
* *Meditate on your inheritance in Christ (Ephesians 1:3–6)*

Dwelling on Things

A counsellee came to see my wife complaining of obsessive thoughts about an incident in her local church. No matter how much she tried praying about them, confessing her sin, telling herself the truth, she could not shake off these constant thoughts. She kept reliving the situation, trying to understand it, but the more she did this, the worse she felt – anxious and very stressed. All psychological symptoms work for us, so Frances investigated what these thoughts were doing for this lady. It turned out that the purpose they were serving was her attempt to justify her part in the situation, and to overcome the guilt she felt over having failed always to do everything "right". By doing this, she felt somehow she could protect herself from the pain of failure. Relief came when she accepted her failure as a fact, along with the pain this brought her, and trusted in God's forgiveness and ability to comfort her. Resisting the pain and guilt had resulted in the obsessive thoughts, and caused more stress.

Get up and get on

In 2 Samuel 12:13–23, we find David, fasting and pleading with God for his baby who was dying. He spent nights lying on the ground and he would not eat any food. "*On the seventh day the child died*" (v. 18). "*Then David got up from the ground. After he had washed, put on lotions and changed his clothes, he went into the house of the Lord and worshipped. Then he went to his own house ... and he ate*" (v. 20). Then David comforted his wife Bathsheba.

So we see that when what he feared happened, despite fasting, David did not dwell on it but got up and got on with his life. It is right, normal and human to grieve and mourn, to repent and learn from what has been happening in our lives. But to go on recriminating and forever trying to get answers is stressful, debilitating, and paralysing. It can keep us from enjoying the rest of our life which God has planned for us. This is a form of self-protection which is a very common cause of stress, wanting to protect ourselves from loss of reputation, identity, blocked goals, failure, guilt and pain etc.

Leave it with God

This must be dealt with by accepting the pain or discomfort and depending upon the Lord Himself to be our protector, our vindicator, and our fortress. *"He who dwells in the shelter of the Most High will rest in the shadow of the Almighty. I will say of the Lord, 'He is my refuge and my fortress, my God, in whom I trust'"* (Psalm 91:1–2). Then we can do away with the past, leave it in God's hands and get on with the present and the future.

Paul says in Philippians 3:13 – *"But one thing I do: Forgetting what is behind and straining towards what is ahead ..."* and to the Ephesians in 4:31–32 *"Get rid of all bitterness, rage and anger, brawling and slander, along with every form of malice."*

For reflection and action:

* Are there things you need to put behind you?
* Are you trying to protect yourself by constantly reanalysing a situation?
* Do you need to accept your part in it and trust in God's forgiveness, cleansing and restoration?
* Should you be getting on with the life that God has planned for you?

Are you stressed because you are snowed under by what you have taken on? The solutions are simple, but you have to be brave enough to put them into effect.

Easing the pressure

1. Stop doing some of the things you are doing. Preferably the non-essential, least important. Experts in time management tell us that we spend 80% of our time on the 20% least important things. Do you really need to do all you are doing? Have you taken time to think about this? Have you prayed about this? Or are you afraid to get off the treadmill?

2. Stop taking on any more, at least before you have thought about it and prayed about it. We learned a good strategy from a friend of ours who is in great demand as a speaker and on committees. Never say "Yes" on the phone at the time you are being asked to do something. This gives you time to discuss with your spouse or family, look at your other commitments, pray about it and then decide whether you should or should not do it.
Jesus, with all the pressures and demands on Him, did not try to do everything and sometimes said "No".

3. If deadlines are a problem, try to leave yourself more time. We hear much about rushing for trains and planes nowadays and meeting deadlines. But we hear little about start times. When possible, try to start earlier for the train or plane, or on the journey, or on the assignment. Then you may not be so rushed.

4. Try to develop greater efficiency. This may mean an investment in time of learning better ways, or of developing time saving systems.

5. Would you rather be effective or efficient? Not much reflection is needed to decide that being effective is more important, though being efficient would also be good. But there is little point in being super-efficient if what you do is not effective. Remember, "Being efficient is doing things right"; "Being effective is doing the right thing".

6. Plan. If you fail to plan you are planning to fail. It is especially important to plan in the important, but not necessarily urgent things – like time with God, with your spouse, your children, friends, building relationships. If you do not plan them ahead you will never find time for them and the urgent will always take up all the time.

Plan with God

Of course you can go on a time management course, but if you are stressed you probably don't have time! Giving time to prayer about how you should be spending your time and utilising these simple suggestions will make you less stressed about time. Are you brave enough to try?

For reflection and action:

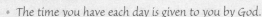

- The time you have each day is given to you by God.
- Are you being a good steward of your time? Have you prayed about this?
- Should you
  - be stopping certain things?
  - not taking on more?
  - starting earlier?
  - be more effective rather than more efficient?

Time Pressures 2

Are you bad at delegating? Delegating is one way of using your own time better and reducing your stress. In Exodus 18, Jethro, Moses' father-in-law, was aware that Moses was taking on too much and was getting stressed. "You and these people who come to you will only wear yourselves out. *The work is too heavy for you; you cannot handle it alone. Listen now to me and I will give you some advice, and may God be with you*" (vv.18–19).

Can you delegate?

Jethro's advice was that Moses should appoint other judges and delegate much of the work to them. "*Have them serve as judges for the people at all times, but have them bring every difficult case to you; the simple cases they can decide themselves. That will make your load lighter, because they will share it with you*" (v. 22). So delegation is a God-honoured principle.

Why not?

There are many reasons why you may not want to delegate: "It would be quicker to do it myself"; "I would do it better myself"; "I would feel guilty for imposing this on others"; "Maybe the one I delegate to will do it better than I could, and I may go down in others' estimation" (Perish the thought!); "If I don't do it, nobody else will do it and it probably won't be done, but people want it to be done."

None of the reasons usually given should be sufficient to deflect you from taking the necessary actions. Yes, it may take longer. But this is an investment of time – not a waste of it. Yes, others may not do it as well – but at least it will be done. And even if it is not perfect, it will probably be good enough.

Why should you feel guilty if others have offered to help. If they do it better, wonderful. You will have the confidence to delegate more in the

"The Lord said to Moses: 'Bring me seventy of Israel's elders who are known to you as leaders and officials among the people … They will help you carry the burden of the people so that you will not have to carry it alone.'" Numbers 11:16–17

future. If no one does it, it won't be done and if others want it to be done so desperately, why don't some of them do it?

You may not have anyone to delegate to, especially at work. What about at home? Could your children do more? The usual retort from mums is, "It's too much hassle. Easier to do it myself". But an investment of time and energy and patience can pay dividends. It's also good for the children to learn to be responsible.

Delegation not only gains you valuable time, but it helps to develop and build up those to whom you delegate. When you delegate, give clear help and instruction and then let them get on with it. Poor delegation can be more stressful than no delegation!

Moses had to be brave enough to delegate. Are you? It might make a difference as to whether you survive or not!

For reflection and action:

- Should you be delegating some of your tasks?
- Are there more important tasks you could be doing with your time?
- You will have to give an account one day of how you used your time.
- Delegation could help you and also those to whom you delegate.

Exaggeration

Have you heard others saying "If that happens it will be the end"? Have you found yourself saying or thinking "This is awful"; "If I have to do that, I'll die"; "I'll never get over this"; "I could never do that"?

Is it really the end of the world?

We would not feel as stressed as often as we do if we did not exaggerate so much, if we did not "awfulise" so often. Will it really be the end? Is it really awful? It may not be very pleasant, it may even be bad. But "the end"?

Exaggerating things can cause you to feel stressed and can also lead you to make hasty decisions; to take foolish and wrong actions.

Even Elijah, that great prophet, acted out of exaggeration. In 1 Kings 19:3 we read that "*Elijah was afraid and ran for his life*". In verse 4 that he sat down under a broom tree and prayed that he might die, and later in verses 13–14 "*Then a voice said to him, 'What are you doing here, Elijah?' He replied, 'I have been very zealous for the Lord God Almighty. The Israelites have rejected your covenant, broken down your altars, and put your prophets to death with the sword. I am the only one left, and now they are trying to kill me too.'*"

The Lord then told him what he should do and then in verse 18 (I like the Living Bible version here) the Lord said "*... and incidentally, there are 7000 men in Israel who have never bowed to Baal nor kissed him.*" We can see how exaggerated Elijah's thinking was and the effect that it had on him.

Another example of exaggeration and the consequences is in Numbers 13. When the spies whom Moses had sent to explore the promised land returned, all but two of them gave a bad report: "*We can't attack those people; they are stronger than we are*" (v.31). "*All the people we saw there are of great size*" (v.32). "*We seemed like grasshoppers in our own eyes, and we looked the same to them*" (v. 33).

> "The people are stronger and taller than we are;
> the cities are large, with walls up to the sky."
> **Deuteronomy 1:28**

"Walls up to the sky"

There is more exaggeration in the same spy story in Deuteronomy 1:28. They reported *"The people are stronger and taller than we are; the cities are large, with walls up to the sky"*. Did they exaggerate or did they exaggerate! And because they did, they were afraid and the Israelites did not enter the land, but wandered for 40 years in the wilderness. What a price to pay for stress and fear brought about by exaggeration.

In Psalm 73 note how the psalmist's thinking and feelings changed once he came before God and saw things from God's perspective.

For reflection and action:

- *Have you been exaggerating the problems in your life at the moment? Do you need to ask God to help you get them in proportion, especially since you are not in them alone and God is with you.*
- *Do you need to stop telling God how big your problems are and start telling your problems how big your God is?*

I Want Out!

Have you felt like getting away to a desert island, wanting out of the situation, wanting the pain of the pressure to stop? Through prayer and God's mercy ways may open up for you to get away, or circumstances may change. But there are times when it is just not possible to leave the problem or pressure behind, sometimes there is no way out. A loved one dies. We may be deserted by a wife or husband. A relationship is broken off. A conflict at work or church shows no sign of resolution. We lose our job. We fail an exam. We develop a chronic illness.

Beware the quick fix

Intractable situations like these can be very stressful but you must beware the quick fix. There may be short-term gains, but long-term consequences. In Genesis 25:29–34, Esau stemmed his hunger quickly by selling his birthright. But there were, and are even today, long-term consequences.

Marrying quickly again after losing your spouse, taking up another relationship on the rebound, may solve the immediate loneliness, but can lead to longer term pain. Immediately resorting to tranquillisers may make you feel that you are coping, but you can get hooked on them. Leaving a job, an area, a church, a marriage, emigrating, may get you away from a difficult situation, but other strains and pressures even worse may overtake you. Rushing into any job when you've lost one may give you something to do, but if it is not what you are trained or suited for, it may prove disastrous. Giving up a potential career because of an exam failure may affect the rest of your life. Although intractable illness can be horrendous, suicide can never be the answer. Even if a quick fix seems to work, it can never be of lasting benefit if it is not God's will.

> **"Blessed is the man who perseveres under trial, because when he has stood the test, he will receive the crown of life that God has promised to those who love him." James 1:12**

Don't miss God's plan

If you are in a difficult time, take time to pray and ask God's guidance for your next move. It may be that God wants you to go through the testing time. He may want you to learn something specific, to refine you, to enrich you or simply to teach you to become more dependent on Him. If you immediately take things into your own hands you may miss God's opportunity and plan for you.

I think it was D.L. Moody who said, "Never give up your ticket in the middle of the tunnel." And if you go through it, you will not do so on your own. God has said, *"Fear not, for I have redeemed you; I have summoned you by name; you are mine. When you pass through the waters, I will be with you; and when you pass through the rivers, they will not sweep over you. When you walk through the fire, you will not be burned; the flames will not set you ablaze. For I am the Lord, your God, the Holy One of Israel, your Saviour"* (Isaiah 43:1–3). So be encouraged. The darkest time is often just before the dawn.

For reflection and action:

* Are you going through pressures and trials?
* Are you tempted to quit, get out, take things into your own hands?
* Are you tempted to sell the future to purchase the present?
* Perhaps God wants you to go through it.

Goals

Have you ever stopped to consider why you are doing what you are doing, for that matter why you do anything? Why do you weed the garden? You may find that you have a few goals or objectives in doing something as simple as that. Everything you do, you do to achieve goals. In some areas it may be more difficult to uncover what your goals are, but goals there are.

What are your goals in your marriage? What about in your church? How do you feel if you achieve your goals? Good, satisfied, at peace. How do you feel if you do not achieve your goals? Frustrated, stressed, anxious, depressed, angry.

What are your goals?

So it is important, if you are not going to get too stressed, that you achieve your goals. But you may be setting yourself goals that you do not have control over. In effect you have set yourself up for failure.

If your goal is church growth and the church grows – wonderful – all good feelings. But if it does not grow – frustration, more work, more prayer, and if still no growth, depression and despair – leading to a possible move, a loss of faith. But do you control – ultimately – whether your church grows or not? You can have a vision for a big church. You can work towards it, but you do not have control over it. You have taken responsibility for something over which you have no ultimate control, and so you have set yourself up. This is an important principle to learn if you are going to avoid stress in many parts of your life. Do not give yourself goals over which you do not have ultimate control.

What is the answer? Obviously to have goals where you do have ultimate control. If you think about this – you will find that there are very few – but don't get depressed. God has the answer.

Your main goal should be to please Him. No one else has control over that but you. "*In everything you do, put God first, and he will direct you and crown your efforts with success*" (Proverbs 3:6, TLB).

> "But seek first his kingdom and his righteousness, and all these things will be given to you as well."
> **Matthew 6:33**

Pleasing God

But how do you know what will please God? In general :

1. Do your best. *"Let everyone be sure that he is doing his very best, for then he will have the personal satisfaction of work well done, and won't need to compare himself with someone else"* (Galatians 6:4, TLB).

2. Do what is right and honest, honourable and ethical without fear or fudging. *"For we are taking pains to do what is right, not only in the eyes of the Lord but also in the eyes of men"* (2 Corinthians 8:21).

3. Follow and obey His commands and advice as laid down in Scripture. *"If you love me, you will obey what I command"* (John 14:15).

So we must study and put into practice what He has told us in His Word about how we should act in all life situations. If you are not sure, pray for wisdom.

For reflection and action:

- *Are certain parts of your life causing stress at this time?*
- *Have you examined your goals in them?*
- *Do you have ultimate control over these goals?*
- *Better to put God first, do your best, do what is right, obey God's Word, leave the outcome to God.*

Regrets, Remorse, Guilt

In our counselling we find that guilt and regrets can be one of the biggest causes of stress. We have all felt guilty and had regrets at some time. We may blame ourselves for a divorce: "I should not have said that; if only I hadn't done this ... etc." We may blame ourselves for the son or daughter who has gone off the rails: "If only I had spent more time with the children, brought them up differently, been less strict; more strict; more loving; more understanding."

If only ...

We may blame ourselves for the financial state we are in: "If only I had been more sensible, listened to better advice." We may blame ourselves for our unemployment: "If only I had changed to another job; stayed in that job; worked harder; I might have got on and not be facing redundancy and unemployment now; if only I had studied more at school or college; if only I had listened to my parents, wife, husband, children, my pastor; if only I hadn't said that; done that; if only I had done better or differently."

There is a good "looking back", when we remember God's faithfulness, goodness and guidance all our lives, but this kind of self-accusation and guilt is a bad "looking back". It can prey on our minds, consciously or subconsciously. It can sap our energy, make us stressed and seriously undermine our ability to cope now.

You are forgiven

As a Christian, if you have repented, there is no need for you to feel guilty anymore. You have been forgiven because Jesus Christ died for you on the cross and His blood has washed away your sins. "*In him we have redemption through his blood, the forgiveness of sins*" (Ephesians 1:7). Why then should you keep reminding yourself when God is saying to you "What sin?"; "What occasion was that?"; "I do not remember it." "*As far as the east is from the*

**"... everyone who believes in him receives forgiveness
of sins through his name."
Acts 10:43**

west, so far has he removed our transgressions from us" (Psalm 103:12). So
you should not be going back to look for them, rehearsing them in your
mind, dusting them off. He has hurled "*all our iniquities into the depths of
the sea*" (Micah 7:19). God has no intention of fishing them out again, and
nor should we.

For reflection and action:

- *Are there things you have done or not done in the past
  which still bother you? They may be stressing you and
  affecting your ability to cope now.*
- *If you have never done so you need to take them to the
  cross, confess them, ask God for forgiveness, and believe
  that you have been forgiven, and like Christian in **Pilgrim's
  Progress**, your burden will roll away. You will be free.*
- *Any time the evil one reminds you of them in the future,
  you can refer him to Jesus who has paid the price of
  forgiveness for you, and you can get on with your life
  without these stressors. "When the devil reminds you
  of your past, you remind him of his future."*

Hard Work Never Killed Anyone, or Did it?

Are you one of the "lucky ones" – still in work? Do you arrive home stressed and exhausted; fall asleep over a meal or TV; have no time or energy for spouse or children, or indeed for anything apart from work? Have you stopped to think of the consequences?

Illnesses and "breakdowns"

I am seeing more and more people who have developed illnesses or "breakdowns" out of the blue. But then I find that the onset was preceded by a period of long and unremitting work, either mental or physical.

A study in America found that individuals under the age of 45 who worked more than 48 hours per week in light industry, had twice the risk of death from coronary heart disease than those who worked no more than 40 hours. Another study of 100 young coronary patients found that 25 had been working in two jobs, another 40 had worked more than 60 hours per week.

"*What does a man get for all the toil and anxious striving with which he labours under the sun? All his days his work is pain and grief; even at night his mind does not rest. This is meaningless*" (Ecclesiastes 2:22–23).

You have a duty to your employer, to give him a good day's work for a fair day's wage. "*Slaves, obey your earthly masters with respect and fear, and with sincerity of heart, just as you would obey Christ*" (Ephesians 6:5). But I do not believe this means that you have to kill yourself with work and for hours that are not part of the contract. Of course there will be times when an extra effort is required, and you may need to work extra hours at certain times of the year. This you can usually cope with and it seldom leads to stress. It's when it becomes the norm that problems arise.

> **"In vain you rise early and stay up late, toiling for food to eat."**
> **Psalm 127:2**

Do you trust God?

Interestingly, the majority of the cases I have seen recently who have become ill after overwork have been self-employed. Are you self-employed and overdoing it because you have to grasp the opportunities, or because you are afraid that you may lose future contracts? Or if employed, because you feel you have to please your employer or otherwise you may lose your job? Or has it simply become a habit? What I hear often is "I have to work this hard." But although it may be a difficult decision, the choice is yours. Is it worth it? For your health and family's sake? "But if I stop working as hard, and the job or the work goes – what then?" We all say that we trust God – but for what?

At seminars we have sometimes asked the questions we heard Dr Larry Crabb putting: "How many of you believe that God is good?" 100% of hands go up. "How many of you believe that God is good enough in whatever situation you are in?" 15–20% of hands go up, and then a few more hesitantly put their hands up. How far are you trusting God with your future? He is good enough.

For reflection and action:

- Are you working too hard?
- Is it worth it?
- What actions are you needing to pray about and discuss with your spouse and family?
- God is good enough, you can trust Him absolutely if you obey.

Misoneism

Do you suffer from misoneism? No, it's not some dread, exotic, tropical disease. It is a fear of anything new or anything novel – in other words "change", and it's stressful. Mark Twain said, "The only people who like change are wet babies." I was taken to task by a midwife when I said this recently at a seminar. "I disagree", she said. "They only like to be changed if they are wet and cold." So Mark Twain and I stand corrected.

I like the sign I heard of over the crèche in a big American church, "We shall not all sleep, but we shall all be changed."

Too much change?

A lot of us, I fear, suffer from misoneism, perhaps especially as we get older. Anything new, any change can stress us. Perhaps we can cope with one change at a time, but if there are a few all at once then it becomes too much for us. We can cope with slow changes, especially if they are so slow we cannot notice them! But if they happen too fast then we cannot cope.

And yet nowadays everything seems to be changing so rapidly: Changes in income tax returns; in state benefits; new bosses; new methods at work; new bank charges; new roads, roundabouts, junctions; new hymns rather than the old favourites; new instruments taking the place of the organ; new seats in place of the pews; new Bible translations; computers, modems, E-mail, the Internet. What changes do they all entail? What do they all mean? Then there are changing values in society, changes in what is accepted and even what is thought of as good.

But whether we like it or not, changes there will be and we will have to live with change. Change is here to stay. The only thing which is constant nowadays is change. How should we respond to it?

Some changes are no doubt for the better and I believe we should welcome and encourage them. Some are neutral, sometimes change for change's sake. Some are bad and as Christians, as salt and light, we should resist them where possible, or speak out against them and pray against them.

Jesus doesn't change

Are you in the middle of changes which are affecting and stressing you? Do they seem to be out of control and running away with you. Then remember: "*Heaven and earth will pass away, but my words will never pass away*" (Matthew 24:35). A verse in one of our old and most-loved hymns says: "Change and decay in all around I see, O thou who changest not, abide with me." What a comfort to know that "*Jesus Christ is the same yesterday and today and forever*" (Hebrews 13:8).

For reflection and action:

- *Are the changes going on in your life good?*
- *Should you be welcoming them?*
- *Are they neutral? Should you be adapting to them?*
- *Are they wrong? Should you be resisting or speaking out against them? Praying against them?*
- *Remember: The "Rock" never changes.*

What is the Point?

Do you ever find yourself thinking or saying to yourself, "What's the point?" It can be stressful if this happens often, or the thought keeps coming back.

There are three distinct occasions when I felt like that. One was when I was absolutely rushed off my feet with no time to relax at all. Another was when life was pretty humdrum or even boring with routine things. And a third when I was having to do things which were decidedly unpleasant.

Then something would happen. A wonderful invitation would come in; a rebate from the Inland Revenue; an encouraging letter; a good school report about the children. Suddenly my spirits would rise and I had forgotten to wonder what was the point of it all. This would last until the next time I was stressed and would catch myself thinking, "What is the point?"

Partial answers

Before I was a Christian, if I stopped to think what the point of it was, I would probably have come up with things like, "I have to make money to live"; "I have to provide for my family"; "I want people to look up to me"; "Fame and fortune await". Not so likely the older I got!

As Christians we know that these are only partial answers, and we feel that we should not have these mood-swing cycles. We know that no matter what good we do, or how well we do it, this will not save us. We are saved by grace alone. So what is the point?

I have had a variety of answers from mature Christians: "It is for you to become more like Jesus; to worship Him, love Him, pray to Him, learn His ways and follow Him; to witness, so that others will come to know Him (and then I thought they too will be asking – "What is the point?"); to be in His plans; to please God; to do everything as unto the Lord."

All these are true, but still I had the question – "What is the point?" Then one day, the Lord put into my hands a book called *Destined for the Throne* by Paul E. Bilheimer. I got my answer. If you have been stressed by this question, then maybe what I learned can help you too.

Preparing to reign with Christ

The point, the reason for all that we do and how we do it, and how we are as Christians, is to prepare us to reign with the Lord in the world to come. The better we are and the better we do what He gives us to do, the greater our reward will be and the greater our responsibility will be in the new earth. Not better as the world knows better, but as Jesus defines better. Yes, as unto the Lord, with joy, without complaining, with love, with patience, with perseverance, at peace. This is the point of it all. "*You have made them to be a kingdom and priests to serve our God, and they will reign on the earth*" (Revelation 5:10).

It has meant a lot to me, as I go about every day in the good times and the bad, to think that everything I do and say, how I do and how I am, matters to Jesus and counts. I hope it may come to be of help to you too.

For reflection and action:

- *Everything you say, do, and think, and how you are today and every day, every moment of every day, matters to Jesus.*
- *It will all determine your place in the new earth.*

Moving on

Have you ever been told, when you are feeling stressed, anxious or depressed, that you should snap out of it? It's very difficult to do, and counsellors are told that they should not say this as it makes things worse. However, I believe there comes a time when you have to, if not snap out of it, at least start taking some control of your future life and move on. I am not referring to situations or events that have come into your life that you will have to go through where you can do little but pray, like bereavement or sickness, but to problems that you can actually do something about.

If you continue to blame it on others, or circumstances, or life, or the evil one, or even God; if you wait either for circumstances to change or for help to come, then you are likely to go on feeling stressed, anxious and depressed.

Start to take control

At the right time and with the needed support, people do best when they start to take control and do something for themselves, as far as their future is concerned.

Encouraging people to start looking at the problems causing the stress, and what they themselves can do about them, can be of great benefit to them. This same technique was used in a study reported in *The British Medical Journal* in 1995. A group of severely depressed patients were divided into three groups. One group was given amitriptylline, a standard antidepressant; another was given a placebo – a dummy pill; and the third group was taught to use a problem-solving technique and how to apply it to their problems. They had a 30-minute session about this weekly for six weeks. At the end of the study, the patients who had used the problem-solving technique had done just as well, in fact possibly better than those on the antidepressant, and both had done better than those on placebo.

> **"Why are you crying out to me? Tell the Israelites to move on."**
> **Exodus 14:15**

I think this is a powerful illustration of the benefits of using something like this technique.

Do something

In Exodus 14, Moses and the children of Israel were stressed and anxious. They had escaped from Egypt but now they were facing the Red Sea with the Egyptian hoards breathing down their necks. The Lord said to Moses *"Why are you crying out to me? Tell the Israelites to move on. Raise your staff and stretch out your hand over the sea to divide the water so that the Israelites can go through the sea on dry ground"* (Exodus 14:15–16).

Both Moses and the Israelites had to do something. When you pray about the situation you are in, don't be surprised if God shows you at the right time and with His direct support, or the support of others, what you should get up and do. Be ready then to move on. He will part the Red Sea.

For reflection and action:

- *Do you need to move on to get out of the stress spiral?*
- *Have you asked the Lord what He wants you to do, and for the courage to do it?*
- *God may already have told you what you should be doing – but you have not yet responded. Ask the Lord to give you the courage to move on.*

Conflicting Commitments

Unless we have a clear idea of what our priorities should be, we will always be left wondering, "Did I make the right choice?", with resultant stress.

God's order of priorities

I believe that God has an order of priorities for us. If we go by His order we will please Him, we have His authority and things will go well for us. I believe the order is God, our spouse, our children, parents and family, work, church activities, "good works", personal interests. Some of these categories may not apply to you, you can leave them out. You may want to add others of your own – like "friends".

Before you violently disagree with such an order let me clarify:

1. This is the "norm" order. Events or circumstances may lead to a *temporary* change. A special assignment at work may need longer hours *for a period*. But in all cases it is important before making a temporary change to pray about it and to discuss it with your spouse, children, family or whoever will be affected.

2. Priority does not mean *necessarily* more time spent. We may spend more time at work, but this does not mean it has top priority. Rather, which is the most important to you? What will normally take precedence?

3. The order may change at different periods of your life, when there are different demands on you.

4. There is a distinct difference between God and church activities. God demands first place – your relationship with Him is what is most important. What you do for the church comes out of that.

5. Men often comment, "I am working long hours, and have to be away from home in my job, but I am doing this for my wife and family." If this is your reasoning, can I suggest you ask your wife or children whether they would rather have the good life or you more at home with them! Don't be surprised at the answer. Are you really doing it for them or because you get your significance from your job?

6. emotional and spiritual health, and they should not be pushed out altogether. However, they are the most flexible and can slip down the order when necessary and can be fitted in around other things.

Keeping to it

When conflicting demands come it is wonderful to be able to fall back on this order of priorities to guide us, knowing that it has God's authority. Although it is sometimes difficult to be brave enough to follow the order, we have found that when we faithfully do, our lives go well.

It is important, too, that even when different demands are not being made on us, we keep to God's order. This is how He has made us, and our lives to function. If we do not, then there can be long-term consequences.

For reflection and action:

- Have you worked out with God's help what God's priorities are in your life? (What would you least like to lose?)
- Are you adhering generally to this order?
- Do you need to reorder your life to bring it into line with God's order?

Give Your Right Brain a Chance

A great and wonderful Creator, I believe, is responsible for designing us. If we follow our Designer's instructions then we have the best hope of living successfully without undue stress.

We are fearfully and wonderfully made and one of the most wonderful parts is our brain. There are two halves which work together, but each half seems to have distinctly different functions.

A degree of balance

Our right brain is the more creative, imaginative, emotional side, whereas the left brain is more analytical, and rational. Obviously we all have two halves and they both function in tandem, but in some people one half tends to dominate. Children are more right-brained than we are. As we get older and life gets earnest and serious, in many of us the left brain seems to dominate. Others, the poets, painters and more emotional people, seem to be more right-brained. Be that as it may, with stress the left brain seems to dominate. It is good if there is a degree of balance between the two hemispheres of our brains and especially with regard to stress.

Right-brain activitites

We can enhance the functioning of the right brain, I believe, by indulging in right-brain activities. Enjoying poetry, painting, music, are all relaxing and engage the right brain. Many busy and stressed leaders have engaged in these right-brain activities and presumably they helped them to relax and cope with the stress in their lives. Sir Winston Churchill painted, Edward Heath had his music, and a number of politicians read and write poetry.

Many people find that listening to good music, either live at concerts or on tape, is uplifting and also decreases tension and stress. You can have music therapy which can alleviate anxiety and stress and be very relaxing.

David's harp playing soothed Saul (1 Samuel 16:23): "*Whenever the spirit from God came upon Saul, David would take his harp and play. Then relief would come to Saul; he would feel better, and the evil spirit would leave him.*" There is an interesting implication here that evil spirits do not like good music and leave! At least this one did!

In times of stress and depression, many have found the Psalms and their poetry soothing, comforting, uplifting and encouraging. Where I was brought up in Scotland, there were not only hymns in every church service, but we sang psalms and paraphrases. Nowadays, the words of some psalms are contained in up-to-date songs and are a wonderful way of remembering these psalms.

St Paul told the Ephesians that they should "*Speak to one another with psalms, hymns and spiritual songs. Sing and make music in your heart to the Lord*" (Ephesians 5:19).

So do not neglect these right-brain pursuits, particularly saying or singing psalms.

For reflection and action:

* *Are you mainly using your left brain?*
* *Do you need to indulge in more right-brained activities?*
* *Meditate on: Psalm 23.*

Worried About the Future? The Key is in the Past

Are you anxious about the future? We know that we should not get stressed or worry about the future. We are told *"Do not be anxious about anything"* (Philippians 4:6).

How can I stop worrying?

How can you stop worrying and being anxious? God recommends a way, and if He recommends it, it must be good. He says, "Look back". Look back and remember how faithful He has been – not just in general, but to you. Remind yourself how He has guided and led you and provided for you, what He has taught you. Has He ever let you down? And thank Him. *"Do not be anxious about anything, but in everything, by prayer and petition, with thanksgiving, present your requests to God"* (Philippians 4:6). When you do this it encourages you, strengthens you, makes you feel better, lets you straighten your shoulders, gives you faith to go on, because He has promised the same care and attention for you for the future.

The Israelites were urged to remember the works that God had done, His miracles and judgements He had pronounced (1 Chronicles 16:12). When they were facing the Red Sea with the Egyptian army pounding after them they were terrified. Would they have been so terrified if they had remembered how God had miraculously brought plagues on the Egyptians but had spared them, and then delivered them from the Egyptians? I wonder.

When Jezebel threatened to kill Elijah, would he have been as afraid and run for his life if he had stopped to think how great his God had been to him, how He had miraculously set fire to the water soaked sacrifice, how the Lord sent the ravens to feed him and had brought the widow's son back to life?

> **"Praise the Lord, O my soul, and forget not all his benefits."**
> **Psalm 103:2**

Count your blessings

When I was a boy in Scotland a favourite paraphrase we sang was: "O God of Bethel, by whose hand thy people still are fed, who through this weary pilgrimage, has all our fathers led." An old hymn says:

When upon life's billows you are tempest tossed,
When you are discouraged thinking all is lost,
Count your many blessings, name them one by one,
And it will surprise you what the Lord hath done.

A practice the Lord encouraged in the Israelites was to erect "Ebenezers" – monuments or memorials to the help God gave them at particular times, such as in the middle of the Jordan, and on the west bank of the Jordan after they had miraculously crossed over. Samuel set up an "Ebenezer" after defeating the Philistines near Mizpeh. One Christian community I heard of kept a glass bowl with marbles in it, each marble representing an answer to prayer or an intervention of the Lord, which was continually being added to.

It is so easy to take the Lord's goodness for granted, and to become focused on what is not happening, or on uncertainties and worries. Having an "Ebenezer" will help build your faith in a mighty God, and prevent those worrying thoughts having full reign in your life.

For reflection and action:

- *Worried about the future? Remind yourself how God has been good to you in so many ways – and praise Him.*
- *Consider having an "Ebenezer" yourself.*

Often we know why we feel anxious or depressed. Something stressful has been happening in our lives to make us feel that way, but sometimes the feelings just seem to come by themselves.

Feeling anxious or depressed

There just might be a physical or medical cause, so if feelings like this are a problem for you, it's a good idea to have a medical check up. Depression may be due to an underactive thyroid, or anaemia. Conditions like these need treatment. At the menopause HRT (Hormone Replacement Therapy) may be a great help for anxiety and depression.

Perhaps you are suffering from SAD – Seasonal Affective Disorder. Depression is much worse in the winter months, especially when the weather is dull. Spring will bring relief and you may be helped by a winter holiday in the sun. If the SAD is really bad, then your doctor may prescribe some time each day under special lights.

But if there does not seem to be any real cause for the stress might there be something else behind it? What we hear or read or watch can change our body chemistry and functioning and affect our feelings. If you watch an exciting film or sporting event on TV, the adrenaline can surge, your pulse race and you feel tense. Reading a newspaper account of a despicable murder, child abuse, or neglect, can make your blood boil, your blood pressure can go up and you feel that you might burst a blood vessel. Listening to a story of heroism or bravery, a child being saved, you can feel a lump in your throat and a tear in your eye and you can feel all warm and good inside.

> **"Whatever is true, ... noble, ... right, ... pure, ... lovely, ... admirable –
> if anything is excellent or praiseworthy – think about such things."**
> **Philippians 4:8**

What are you thinking about?

Research has shown that if we feed "hate" words – words like anger, blame, unhappiness, anxiety, tension, agitation – to subjects while they are exercising, their heart rate, blood pressure, oxygen consumption and stress hormones all increase more than if they are fed "love" words – like joy, praise, happiness, relaxation, calmness. Incidentally, in the English language there are about twice as many "hate" words as "love" words.

Every day the TV brings right into our living rooms news of hate and terrorism and war from the Middle East, Northern Ireland, Africa, Europe. There are sickening reports on TV and in our newspapers of murder, rape, abuse, violence, burglary. Horror films, thrillers and conflict discussions and arguments seem to outnumber the uplifting programmes and be more popular.

Perhaps there is little wonder that fed a diet of such things and given what we know about how they affect us, that we can experience stress and an undercurrent of anxiety and depression. While TV can be educational and we should be aware of our world and how we can be salt and light, we should be aware of the effect our reading and viewing has on us.

We should take time to read God's Word, listen to good music, and uplifting stories. In short, we should take St Paul's advice seriously about what we should be filling our minds with.

For reflection and action:

- *Is your daily reading and viewing uplifting?*
- *Do you need to change the balance?*

Our Rights

"Demand your rights!" "I have a right to be given, to get, to withhold, to be heard, to be recognised." "Because they have, then I should have too." "Why should I help, give, give in?"

Demandingness has become a way of life, but demanding your rights and making sure you get them is very stressful. It's even more stressful if you feel that you have not been given them. Demandingness is at the root of much of the trouble between countries, between groups, at work, in communities, in families, between husband and wife. Demandingness leads to wars, to terrorism, to strikes, to division, to feuds and to divorce. If you become involved in any of this, it can be very stressful for you, and anger, bitterness and resentment can soon follow.

Selfishness

Lack of communication is one of the big causes of marriage breakdown, separation and divorce, but at the heart of very many of the tragic cases we see is selfishness or demandingness.

One of the great box office song hits was *I Did it My Way*. This way of thinking and behaving is bad for relationships and peace of mind, but the stress involved is also bad for our health.

The Lord Jesus knew that it is bad for us. When two of His disciples wanted the important places in the kingdom, Jesus told them "... *whoever wants to become great among you must be your servant, and whoever wants to be first must be your slave – just as the Son of Man did not come to be served, but to serve ...*" (Matthew 20:26–28).

In Matthew 5:39–41, Jesus says, "*I tell you, Do not resist an evil person. If someone strikes you on the right cheek, turn to him the other also. And if someone wants to sue you and take your tunic, let him have your cloak as well. If someone forces you to go one mile, go with him two miles. Give to the one who asks you, and do not turn away from the one who wants to borrow from you."*

In Matthew 20:1–16 we read the parable that Jesus told about the landowner who agreed to pay men a set sum of money for working in his vineyard, and how those who worked all day felt that they should have been paid more than those who worked for only one hour.

Leave it with the Lord

Are you in a situation where you are demanding your rights, where well-meaning friends are advising you to pursue them? Make no mistake, there will be a cost. You may obtain your rights, but it could be at the price of stress and damage to your health – mental, physical and spiritual. The Lord knows your situation. He has a better plan than you getting your rights. Better by far to put it in His hands and leave the outcome to Him. That way lies peace. The Holy Spirit can provide you with the strength and grace to do this. Why not ask Him now?

For reflection and action:

- *Have you been demanding your rights?*
- *Are you bitter because you have not received them?*
- *Are you being selfish?*
- *All we have is from God. It is His to give and to take away. He is big enough to see to it that justice is done when He wills.*

Humour

If you have recently been bereaved or suffered a serious setback, then there may be little in your life at the moment to laugh about. But even when things are going well and there is nothing to cry about, has life become so serious that you have no time for anything unless it is deadly serious? Have you stopped seeing the funny side of things?

Laughter – the best medicine

Laughter reduces our stress levels and is good not only for our emotional and mental health, but for our physical health too. Norman Cousins was suffering from cancer. He believed that if he laughed enough, the chemical and hormonal changes in his body could cure his cancer. He bought and rented as many comedy films that he could get hold of and watched them and laughed for hours on end. Sure enough – his cancer was cured.

In a recent study, two groups of people were given very intricate problems to solve. But before they attempted the problems, one group was asked to watch a quite harrowing documentary video, while the other watched a comedy film. The group who had watched the comedy performed much better at the problem solving than the group who had watched the documentary.

Have you ever noticed even when people are tense or stressed, the arrival of a baby or young child on the scene can make everyone smile and somehow the stress goes out of the situation.

Smile – Jesus loves you

I liked the sticker, popular some years ago, which said, "Smile, Jesus loves you". We do have a lot to smile about, to be happy about.

Demos Shakarian who founded the Full Gospel Businessmen's Fellowship entitled his book about his vision for reaching businessmen through dinners, *The Happiest People On Earth*. This title is based on the premise

> ### "A cheerful heart is good medicine."
> ### Proverbs 17:22

that God has a purpose for all His children and has gifted and created them with all they need to fulfil that purpose, therefore they should be the happiest people on earth because they are fulfilling their created purpose.

Not only that, but God Himself is the primary source of our joy, and we will experience this as a fruit of the Spirit (Galatians 5:22), and 1Thessalonians 1:6 states, "... *in spite of severe suffering, you welcomed the message with the joy given by the Holy Spirit*". The Bible reveals that we do not need to rely on an external cause for joy and happiness, but that we can receive it directly from God Himself – "*May the God of hope fill you with all joy and peace as you trust in him, so that you may overflow with hope by the power of the Holy Spirit*" (Romans 15:13).

For reflection and action:

* "*A cheerful look brings joy to the heart*" (Proverbs 15:30).
* Do you need to lighten up a bit?
* Should you be smiling more?
* Why do you not laugh more?
* Should you be seeking more of the fruit of the Spirit?

Rest

In the busiest week the universe has ever seen, God rested on the seventh day. He did not have to rest. He does not get tired. He never sleeps. Moreover, being an all-powerful God, He did not need to take six days to do His creation work. He could have done it all in the twinkling of an eye. Why then did He take so long and why did He rest? He did it as a pattern for us to follow – "*Remember the Sabbath day by keeping it holy ... For in six days the Lord made the heavens and the earth, the sea, and all that is in them, but he rested on the seventh day. Therefore the Lord blessed the Sabbath day and made it holy*." (Exodus 20:8,11).

Many of the cases of burnout or stress we see have been busy seven days each week. I believe that when God says "rest", He means rest – ceasing from our labours – not relaxation, or sport or hobbies. We need these too, but they are not necessarily restful. I believe God means rest and not DIY, or gardening or car washing, though we need time for these too. We need a day in the week when what we do physically and mentally is reduced to a minimum, with as few responsibilities as possible. Work demands it, and yet it has been shown that time spent working beyond 40 hours per week results in time spent that is increasingly unproductive.

Doing nothing

You may find it difficult to do nothing. You may even feel guilty. There are many excuses why you must be busy seven days in the week. "I would never get everything done." It takes courage to stop on a Sunday but my experience, and that of others who do, has been that, surprise, surprise, we are better able to cope during the rest of the week and "miraculously" all gets done that needs to be done in the other six days.

"How can I as a housewife and mother possibly rest on a Sunday?" There will be some work that has to be done we know, but it can be reduced to a minimum. When our children were young, we stopped cooking Sunday lunch and either had sandwiches or prepared it on Saturday. The washing up was left or put in the dishwasher. You need to be inventive to fit in with your own situation.

A day of rest

If you are in one of the caring professions, are a shift worker, self-employed or in the ministry, then I believe it is crucial that you observe this instruction from your Maker. You may have to work on Sunday. You need another day of rest in the week over and above the time needed for gardening, DIY, housework and hobbies.

I believe this is how God has made us to function. He knows we need the rest. You may ignore this, but there may be a price to pay.

For reflection and action:

- Are you having one day of rest in the week? God has said it is important. The Sabbath was made for man, not man for the Sabbath. It is one of the Ten Commandments. If you broke one of the other commandments, would you not feel that you had sinned and needed to repent and change? So what is different about this commandment?
- Are you brave enough to obey? You will be blessed by the Lord for honouring Him.

The Biggest Stressor Today? 1

I think the stressor that affects more people than any other, and causes most stress, is insecurity or uncertainty. When you feel secure you can relax, and get on with your life. But if you feel insecure, you can become anxious, worried, fearful and stressed about the future. You will probably find it difficult to make decisions.

Insecurity

To feel secure you need to know that what you are depending on for your security is absolutely dependable. It is often when we find out that something is not dependable that we realise how much we were depending on it for our security. When something or someone you are depending on proves undependable, you feel shaken, let down, even betrayed. Will you ever be able to trust them, or anybody, again?

But we all need to feel secure. We are born with this need, and I believe it is a God-given need. There was a time when people did feel more secure; when things were more dependable, but no longer.

Many still depend on their job for security and if they become redundant, security goes and anxiety and stress follow. It is well known in stress research that ever since the time of high unemployment in the 1930s, redundancy and unemployment are stressful and associated with a higher risk of death, illness and psychological ill health. But even before redundancy comes, the fear of it and the insecurity that goes with the uncertainty can have similar effects.

Some time ago a large group of male and female civil servants who were in a department threatened with privatisation were compared with another group in a department where no threat existed. There was a marked deterioration in the health of the group under threat compared with the "secure" group.

> **"My people have committed two sins: They have forsaken me, the spring of living water, and have dug their own cisterns, broken cisterns that cannot hold water." Jeremiah 2:13**

How dependable is any job now? You can be privatised, nationalised, rationalised, be taken over, be downsized, outplaced, or whatever the current euphemism is for being made redundant.

What do you depend on?

You may depend on other things – your pension – then you hear of dishonesty or mismanagement in the pension funds and you begin to wonder, "is mine safe?"

Safe as houses. People depended on their house for security – then came the property market collapse. Safe as the Bank of England. Then you remember devaluation and the European currency collapses, the BICC collapse, the Barings Bank collapse, and wonder.

Perhaps you had been depending on your wife or husband, and they've gone. Separation and divorce is so common nowadays. Perhaps you have been depending on your church or pastor for encouragement and support; but people are found to have feet of clay and you feel disillusioned and hurt.

We will look further at this tomorrow and at the answer – the only truly dependable source of security.

For reflection and action:

- *Do you feel insecure, fearful of the future?*
- *What are you depending on for your security?*
- *Are these sources utterly dependable?*

I remember counselling an NHS manager who was very stressed. He was working harder and harder to keep up and was getting very fatigued. I asked him to consider the sources of his security and he quickly realised that none of his sources was entirely dependable. "This is very depressing!" he said.

"Good", I thought, "I'm getting through to him."

"Well, at least I can depend on myself."

"Really? You can stop becoming ill? You can depend on living to retirement age? You can depend on living at all?"

He got the point and then the question I had been waiting for. "So what's the answer? I need to feel secure, but what or whom can I depend on? Is there nothing or nobody?"

"Would you like to feel absolutely secure?" I asked. "Of course!" he said.

Security in God

Are you stressed because your security has been taken away, or is being threatened, or may be in the future? Have you realised that the sources you are relying on are utterly undependable, and this has made you feel even more vulnerable and anxious? God is the answer, as He is to everything. He is the only person who is entirely dependable and has made us to get our security from Him. If you put your trust in Him, you are guaranteed absolute security.

You are safe in Him

He has the whole world in His hands. Not only that, but He has you in His hands. You are safe and secure if you trust Him with every aspect of your future. If He is capable of saving you from hell, surely He is capable of looking after the rest of your future.

> **"Look at the birds of the air; they do not sow or reap or store away in barns, and yet your heavenly Father feeds them. Are you not much more valuable than they?"**
> **Matthew 6:26**

Jesus said *"Do not worry about tomorrow, for tomorrow will worry about itself. Each day has enough trouble of its own"* (Matthew 6:34). He does not say this so that we will put our heads in the sand, or not be sensible about our future, but because we need not worry about tomorrow if we are actually trusting Him. He also said *"Consider the ravens: They do not sow or reap, they have no storeroom or barn; yet God feeds them. And how much more valuable you are than birds! Who of you by worrying can add a single hour to his life? Since you cannot do this very little thing, why do you worry about the rest?"* (Luke 12:24–26).

We are secure if we have built on the Rock. *"Therefore everyone who hears these words of mine and puts them into practice is like a wise man who built his house on the rock. The rain came down, the streams rose, and the winds blew and beat against that house; yet it did not fall, because it had its foundation on the rock. But everyone who hears these words of mine and does not put them into practice is like a foolish man who built his house on sand. The rain came down, the streams rose, and the winds blew and beat against that house, and it fell with a great crash"* (Matthew 7:24–27).

If you have built on the Rock, then you can be sure that if storms of life come, they may beat against you, but you need not fear because you are secure.

For reflection and action:

- *What are your sources of security? Are they dependable?*
- *Only God is fully dependable. Are you building your life on the Rock?*

Each title 99p each

Previously published as the New Perspectives series.

Reducing the Stress Factor
Learn how to deal with stress biblically and effectively.
ISBN: 1-85345-217-3

Facing up to Financial Crisis
Learn how to deal with finances from a biblical perspective.
ISBN: 1-85345-214-9

Living with a Long-term Illness
Discover how to also live in the truth that "...in all things
God works for the good of those who love Him."
ISBN: 1-85345-222-X

Overcoming Redundancy
Face this difficult time by taking the initiative and celebrating
your God-given gifts. ISBN: 1-85345-216-5

A Way out of Despair
Address issues of despair, including suicide, rejection, guilt,
self-hate. ISBN: 1-85345-218-1

Encouraging Carers
This book helps carers to understand that their strength can be
found in God. ISBN: 1-85345-219-X

Building a Better Marriage
A helpful aid for people experiencing a difficult patch, or more
serious issues in their marriage. ISBN: 1-85345-213-0

A Way through Depression
Biblical wisdom to help anyone suffering from this debilitating
condition. ISBN: 1-85345-221-1